My First
Scottish Gaelic
Things Around Me at Home

Picture Book with English Translations

Published By: AuthorUnlock.com

leabaidh

Bed

plaide

Blanket

bobhla

Bowl

brat-ùrlair

Carpet

cùirtearan

Curtains

forc

Fork

biona

Garbage Bin

glainne

Glass

iarann

Iron

siuga

Jug

coire

Kettle

sgian

Knife

glas

Lock

sgàthan

Mirror

muga

Mug

àmhainn

Oven

dealbh

Picture

cluasag

Pillow

truinnsear

Plate

mullach

Roof

siota

Sheet

sgeilp

Shelf

siabann

Soap

sòfa

Sofa

spàin

Spoon

taigh-beag

Toilet

tubhailt

Towel

Printed in Poland
by Amazon Fulfillment
Poland Sp. z o.o., Wrocław

64326661R00019